Preface

This book discusses various methods that are commonly used to objectively assess the fundamental value of real estate. It provides a brief explanation of how the real estate market is affected by the country's interest rates, the unemployment rate, and the overall economic cycle. This book then explains why it is often more lucrative for a borrower to opt for a variable-rate mortgage instead of a fixed-rate mortgage, and how a borrower can request to adjust the terms of their mortgage contract so that it is a more favorable arrangement for the borrower. The aim is to encourage both investors and speculators to approach real estate as a long-term investment, and in this respect, it provides an avenue for prospective buyers to examine this decision with a mindset that is as objective as possible.

Real estate tends to evoke a highly emotional response with many home buyers, and these emotions tend to run high in part due to the large sums of money and large amounts of debt that are involved with this type of purchase. For this reason, it is crucial for the buyer to step back and thoroughly assess their investment without being distracted by all of the subjective, uninformed, and highly irrational opinions which do nothing but create unnecessary noise and confusion.

Real Estate Valuation

The Mechanics of Market Prices

The price adjustment mechanism links each seller with a buyer so that all available inventories can be sold regardless of market trends. If the market was somehow restricted by a governing body, the price mechanism will still exist, however it would be out of step with inventory.

For example, let us suppose that a government with good intentions decides that it would like milk to be affordable for all of its poorest citizens, so by popular demand, the price is mandated by law to be 50 cents per gallon. If the true cost of production for the milk producers is $3 per gallon, then this market is considered to be out of balance with its price. The result is that the milk producers will cease production, and this will create an acute milk shortage, which will quickly drive the true price much higher.

From this example, it can be seen that prices are crucial in communicating to producers what they should produce and how much. At the same time, prices also communicate to consumers what to consume and how much. Ignoring the obvious political and ethical ramifications that are inherent in this rather extreme example, suffice it to say that the price of any inventory can and will swing as needed in order to accommodate any fluctuations in the short-term supply and/or demand for that product. Real estate is no exception to this rule.

Shifts in Property Prices

With real estate, at any given point in time, the vast majority of properties are actually not for sale, and as such, they are not on the market. The only units that are on the market are the relatively small group that is listed for sale. For the buyers, the only price that is relevant in determining the fair market value is the price at which the latest buyer has agreed to purchase the property from the seller. This is because an asset is only worth what others are willing to pay for it at that moment in time.

The latest average transaction price is usually broadcast to all buyers, all sellers, and also to the masses who are not actively buying or selling. When there are more buyers than sellers, this puts upward pressure on the transaction prices. When there are more sellers than buyers, this puts downward pressure on the transaction prices. Market prices are always determined by these two groups, that is, the buyers and sellers.

One interesting fact about buyers and sellers is that most observers tend to over-estimate how large these groups are. In certain circumstances, sudden price movements pertaining to a small number of transactions can very quickly trigger unexpected behaviour in the vast majority who were previously not actively involved in buying or selling.

When large clusters of people from the vast majority decide to react to price triggers, they often rush into the market, inundating the normally small groups of buyers and sellers. The market then becomes highly irrational and the new participants exhibit conformist, or herd behaviour, sometimes referred to by economists as "animal spirits". During a bull market, this results in large numbers of panicked buyers, very few sellers, and rapid price increases, as everyone seeks easy profits. During a bear market, this results in large numbers of panicked sellers, very few buyers, and rapid price decreases, as everyone seeks to avoid losses.

It should be noted and emphasized that the catalyst which sparks the change in direction of prices from upward to downward or vice versa can be astoundingly trivial. The price determination mechanism can be both fragile and frivolous, as it only takes one individual unexpected transaction to cause a massive shift. At an unpredictable moment in time, as soon as the price reaches an unbearable limit, the balance of buyers and sellers will tip, and this will reverse the direction of prices.

The longer the prices have been rapidly moving in any given direction, the greater the probability that the change in direction will elicit a panicked response by clusters of people from the masses that are normally uninvolved in buying or selling.

Risk versus Return

If somebody offered an investment opportunity that pays a return on investment of 9%, is that a good investment? Nine percent sounds like a good return, because banks accounts offer much less, as do bonds. Stocks are often quoted as providing long term rates of return in the 7%-9% range, so this sounds like something as rewarding as a stock. But what if the risk inherent in this investment was closer to 24%? This would mean that the 9% return is being offered with 24% risk, meaning it's a horrible investment opportunity. This is because the investment is risky and so the return on such an investment should be commensurate with that level of risk. So what is risk? And how is it calculated?

Risk can be thought of as the risk of losing an investment either in part or entirely. For example, an investor might buy a stock in a company, and then if that company goes bankrupt, the investor will lose their entire investment. One might think of the rate of return as a very broad guideline that indicates how often that asset class tends to result in a complete loss. For example, a retail credit card lending company might find that 18% of its credit card users go bankrupt rather than repay their credit card debt, and so they may charge an interest rate of 20% to reflect the cost of this form of investment, and to recuperate these losses.

For the purposes of real estate investing, it is not necessary to use a complex formula to figure out what the risk is. Instead, it helps to look at this investment as being within an "asset class". It is the asset class which usually indicates the underlying long-term risk. Over the short-term, anything can happen to a price. A stock price can triple in 3 weeks, and a house price can double in 4 years. But over the long-term, most assets will revert to the average long-term rate of return, according to the asset class to which they belong. The following are some general guidelines for what risk is inherent with different asset classes over the long-term.

1%-2% Federal Government Bonds
3%-6% High Interest Savings Accounts
5%-8% Urban Residential Real Estate
7%-9% Stock Market Index
14%-28% Retail Credit Lending
20%-40% Venture Capital

By looking at the property as a part of an investment portfolio, in the urban residential real estate asset class, the expected risk of 5% to 8% can shed some light onto what kind of return should be expected over the long run. By knowing this, it is possible to then delve further into the valuation, and figure out what kind of price would be reasonable for the property in question.

Price/Earnings Ratio

As with any investment, the owner would like to earn a return on investment that is consistent with the underlying level of risk. This is commonly done by calculating the return on investment, which is the money earned as a percentage of the total amount invested. Even if a buyer has no intention to rent their property to a tenant, performing an assessment of the potential rental earnings can be helpful in assess a property's value from the perspective of an investor.

Let us consider a hypothetical example. Suppose the price of a home is $120,000. This home, or another home that is similar in size, quality, and location, can be rented out to a tenant for $1,000 per month. This means that annual rent is $12,000 per year. The return on investment in this case is 10% per year, which is calculated by dividing the annual rent by the price. $12,000 divided by $120,000 times 100 is equal to 10%.

Investors often calculate the inverse version of this value in order to determine the price to earnings ratio of their investment. The basic price to earnings ratio in this case is 10, which is calculated by dividing the price by the annual rent, or $120,000 divided by $12,000 which equals 10.

To be more thorough, any other costs involved in obtaining this investment, such as land transfer taxes or legal fees should be subtracted from the price, and any mortgage interest and property taxes paid throughout the year should be subtracted from the annual rent amount in order to figure out a more accurate price to earnings ratio. Some investors will then subtract the country's inflation rate from the price to earnings ratio, in this case, bringing it from 10 to 8, assuming a 2% inflation rate.

According to many savvy investors, an investment, including a home, is not worth buying if the final price to earnings ratio is 18 or more. From the seller's perspective, it would often be considered not worth selling a home if the price to earnings ratio is less than 14. Many informed real estate investors therefore gravitate towards buying or selling homes at a price to earnings ratio between 14 and 18 under normal market circumstances. The reason why they tend to buy homes when the price to earnings ratio is around 14 or lower is because they see an opportunity to profit based on the rent they could earn. They tend to sell homes when the ratio is around 18 or higher because for those houses, the rent is not high enough to make a reasonable profit. Even for buyers who will not rent their house to a tenant, this valuation dynamic should be considered, because many buyers within an active real estate market will indeed use this profit analysis to decide whether or not to purchase a property. The more numerous these types of profit-oriented buyers are within a market, the more this valuation method has the potential to affect local prices.

When the ratio for most homes in a city is higher than 18, this is often referred to as a seller's market, which means that the sellers are at an advantage. When the ratio for most homes in a city is lower than 14, this is often referred to as a buyer's market, which means that the buyers are at an advantage.

Please note that this method of valuation is only one of several methods that one can use as a basic guide to figure out the value of a home, and it is not intended to stand alone in determining a price.
There are many other qualitative factors that will determine a home's value, such as supply vs demand, transit infrastructure, interest rates, neighborhood income levels, future prospects, future population growth, foreign investment, the pervasiveness of property speculation, etc. Also, many home buyers are willing to tolerate an abnormally high price to earnings ratio because they intend to live in, rather than to rent out, their home, so this valuation method may not reflect every property market at every point in time.

Price/Income Ratio

This ratio can provide an indication of whether or not a market's property prices are affordable to local buyers, and therefore sustainable. For this method, the home price is compared with the total household income of the general population within that property market.

In the United States, one common measure is the affordability index. If this index is 100, this means that a median income household earns just enough income to buy a median-value home. This assumes that 25% of total gross income is being paid on the mortgage, and that 20% is paid as a down payment. An index greater than 100 means that the local incomes are high enough for the residents to afford homes. An index less than 100 means that incomes are not high enough to afford homes.

A simpler alternative to this affordability index is the price to income ratio. This ratio is equal to the house price divided by total gross household Income. This guideline states that one should not buy a home that costs more than three times the gross household income. If this ratio is less than 3, then the household is likely able to afford the home. If this ratio is greater than 3, then the household may struggle to afford the home. As this ratio approaches 7, the household will likely spend most of their income exclusively on the mortgage, resulting in a situation referred to as being "house poor".

Let us consider a hypothetical example, where the price of a home is $840,000. The total gross income earned by the couple who is considering buying the home is $120,000 per year. The price to income ratio in this case is $840,000 divided by $120,000, which equals 7. A more affordable price for this couple would be triple their income, or $120,000 multiplied by 3, which equals $360,000.

From the perspective of the real estate market as a whole, the same calculation is performed for every property, or for the average property that is for sale, and the average income of the prospective home buyers. This can provide an objective indication of whether homes are over-priced or under-priced for the local residents.

Vacancy Rate

The vacancy rate is a helpful metric which measures the amount of property in a city that is not occupied by anybody. The vacancy rate is equal to the total available units divided by all units in the property market in question. A rate of zero would mean that all housing units are occupied.

A vacancy rate of 5% or less indicates that the supply is very close to demand. In this situation, rental units can be difficult to find, and so rents will likely be high. Also, this can contribute to upward pressure on property prices, which can be profitable for real estate investors and landlords.

During prolonged housing booms, there is sometimes a tendency to over-build real estate due to speculation that prices will continue to rise. This has occurred in the past few decades in Spain, Japan, the United States, and China, as well as in several other countries.

If the vacancy rate climbs higher than 5%, this indicates that there is likely an over-supply of rental units. As the vacancy rate increases, this normally results in lower rents, and downward pressure on property prices. If this situation persists, real estate investors and landlords run the risk of being exposed to reduced profits or even losses.

It is important to note that if prices rise quickly in a city and the vacancy rate rises quickly as well, then this is a warning sign that the high prices might not reflect the fundamental value of the homes. In the most extreme cases, entire neighborhoods or groups of developments can remain unoccupied for extended periods of time, and this is often referred to as a "ghost city".

Signs of a Market Bubble

There are some warning signs which tend to be indicative of the development of a real estate bubble. These indicators can be found in most types of asset pricing bubbles and this phenomenon can gradually occur in any market. Potential investors should be mindful of these signs whenever markets appear to be behaving irrationally.

Warning signs can persist over long periods of time, and it is not possible to accurately and consistently predict the timing of the end of asset bubbles, aside from guessing. It is often said that "markets can remain irrational longer than investors can remain solvent," meaning that it is neither advisable nor feasible to attempt to profit by guessing the timing of the market's fluctuations.
The following is a list of some of the developments which often occur with asset bubbles. Please note that the events do not necessarily unfold in the order that they are listed below.

- The investment is initially considered to be difficult to obtain.
- The earliest buyers earn large profits and are very vocal about it.
- There is increased interest in the investment opportunity, and an increase in demand for the media to broadcast success stories pertaining to it.
- Bystanders who struggle to afford the increasingly expensive investment fear that they will miss out on an opportunity to earn wealth quickly.
- New investors demand more flexible financing in order to participate.
- Banks become willing lenders for investors who normally would not qualify for similar investment loans.
- Investors believe that the growth will continue, and they become uninterested in the sustainability of profits,

- or in the underlying investment's earnings, which for housing takes the form of rent.
- Traditional performance-indicating metrics, such as the price-to-earnings ratio, are deemed to be obsolete.
- Fraud and irregular transaction practices surrounding the popular investment opportunity become more commonplace.
- Investors seek to earn profits quickly, primarily by selling to future investors at increasingly higher prices. This is often referred to as "flipping," or to economists as "The Greater Fool Theory."
- Prices unexpectedly fall, triggering denial at first, followed by panicked selling and falling prices.

Occasionally, excessive levels of property speculation can drive prices so unsustainably high that real estate investments can become extremely risky, and this is referred to as a housing bubble. In order to help mitigate against potential swings in home prices, one helpful rule of thumb is for the homeowner to ensure that their total housing costs are less than 30% of the gross household income, and to keep the total debt costs less than 40% of the gross household income.

Mortgage Clauses Which Protect The Bank During Downturns

Since mortgage lenders are aware of the risks associated with real estate, there is a potentially dangerous clause that is often hidden in the mortgage contract. Borrowers should be fully aware of all clauses in all contracts that they enter into, however this clause in particular should be noted by the borrower, due to its far-reaching implications.

Some lenders include a clause which may require the borrower to make large payments if the property value falls below a threshold. This means that the borrower could be forced to make large unexpected payments to the bank if their home value drops. If the borrow cannot or does not make these required payments, then they could be forced to sell the home at a low price in order to try to pay back the full mortgage all at once, as required by the contract. This also means that many over-leveraged borrowers could lose their homes, as well as some of their home equity, if the housing market experiences price decreases. As the saying goes, "Buyer Beware!" Borrowers who do not have this clause in their contract should still be aware of it, because it could exacerbate a market correction, as the affected home owners might be forced to sell more and more due to this potentially market de-stabilizing clause. The lender might call this the "trigger point", or possibly a different name in the contract. Specifically, it can affect borrowers as follows.

For conventional mortgages with a down-payment of at least 20%, when the market value of the property drops below 80% of the deferred interest plus the outstanding principal, the borrower is given 1 month to either make a lump sum payment to bring the balance down to the appropriate trigger point, or prove that the property value has increased to 80% of the mortgage. For insured or high ratio mortgages with a down payment of less than 20%, when the deferred interest plus the outstanding principal is greater than 105% of the market value of the property, the borrower is given 1 month to either make a lump sum payment to bring the balance down to the appropriate trigger point, or convert to a fixed rate mortgage, or increase the regular monthly payment amount.

The following is a real-life example of the wording that was found in a North American mortgage contract, for a major international bank which shall remain nameless.

Conventional Mortgages (>=20% down payment):
If at any time the outstanding Principal amount (including deferred interest) exceeds 80% of the fair market value of the mortgage property as determined by the lender (with or without an appraisal/valuation), such amount being the "trigger point", the lender will give the borrower notice of such excess (the "trigger

excess") and within 30 days of receiving that notice the borrower must do one of the following:

    1. make a lump sum payment at least equal to the amount of the trigger point excess; or

    2. satisfy the lender that the outstanding principal amount (including deferred interest) does not exceed 80% of the fair market value of the mortgaged property as established by a qualified real estate appraiser approved in writing by the lender, but at the borrower's expense.

If the borrower fails to comply, the lender has the option of demanding repayment in full of the outstanding principal amount (including deferred interest), plus unpaid interest, costs, charges and expenses that the borrower owes under the mortgage agreement and enforcing payment under the mortgage.

Insured aka high ratio mortgages (< 20% down payment):
If at any time the outstanding principal amount (including deferred interest) exceeds 105% of the original advance amount (the "trigger point"), the lender will give notice of such excess (the "trigger excess") and within 30 days of receiving that notice the borrower must do one of the following:

    1. pay the lender a lump sum to reduce the outstanding principal amount by an amount at least equal to the amount of the trigger point excess; or

    2. agree with the lender to convert the mortgage loan to a fixed rate mortgage loan or;

    3. increase the amount of each regular principal and interest payment to an amount sufficient to amortize the outstanding principal amount (including deferred interest) over the remaining amortization period.

If the borrower fails to comply, the lender has the option of demanding repayment in full of the outstanding principal amount (including deferred interest), plus unpaid interest, costs, charges and expenses that the borrower owes under the mortgage agreement and enforcing payment under the mortgage.

Real Estate and the Economic Cycle

Interest Rates

It is important for real estate investors to understand the relationship between what causes interest rates to rise and fall, and how this relates to property values. A question that is often asked by prospective buyers is "Why do interest rates go up and down?" One common misconception is that the government changes the interest rate in order to maintain control of the stock market or the housing market. Although they maintain an acute awareness of these fluctuations and the risks that they pose to the overall economy, central banks do not adjust interest rates according to the housing or stock markets. Instead, they adjust interest rates according to the country's rate of inflation.

The government can stimulate the economy using two methods, which are fiscal stimulus and monetary stimulus. Fiscal stimulus is when the government injects money into the economy by spending money on programs. An example of this would be the building of a highway. Monetary stimulus is when a central bank adjusts the prime interest rate so that companies and citizens borrow more and presumably spend this borrowed money in the economy. An example of this is when the prime rate is lowered after a recession has begun.

Boom and Bust Cycles

The tendency to use monetary policy to keep inflation under control has become the norm because of major problems with inflation that persisted on and off over the past few centuries. These inflationary problems were caused by many factors, including wars, lack of economic oversight, and increased government spending.

Since the time when currencies were introduced centuries ago, it has been seen time and time again that governments tend to have a propensity to inflate their currencies by stimulating the economy in the wrong ways and/or at the wrong times. After the Second World War, Keynesian economic theory became the most prominent driver of government policy, and it tends to be used very heavily and predictably by most modern economists and governments.

In a nutshell, Keynesian economics attempts to soften the effects of the regular economic boom-and-bust cycle by stimulating the economy during recessions and removing stimulus during economic expansion. This economic theory basically visualizes the economy like a car's engine. In this analogy, currency is the fuel, human resources are the engine's oil, and the government is the driver. The engine can be accelerated by "giving it more gas". It can be decelerated by "taking the foot off the gas." It can be slowed down by "applying the brakes". It can overheat if there's not enough oil. This engine analogy and car expressions are very frequently used by the central bank and by the news media to describe what is currently happening to the economy.

Target Rate of Inflation

With the engine analogy in mind, the central bank currently works according its government mandate to control inflation. Central banks are focused on keeping inflation at a low target rate of about 1%-2% per year, and they do this by primarily keeping a close eye on the unemployment rate. If the unemployment rate drops too low, this means that there is not enough "slack" in the labor market, and the economy is said to be overheating. When an economy grows too quickly, companies begin to notice that there are shortages of certain inputs, such as energy, raw materials, or workers.

When there are not enough workers available to do the jobs that are necessary, companies are forced to raise wages in order to attract workers, and in the short-term, this is considered to be beneficial, however if this continues, then prices are driven up as well. The reason why prices are driven up so heavily by wages is because for many companies, one of the largest expenses is the salaries of their employees. This wage and price increase can develop into a self-perpetuating cycle, where they keep rising at an incremental rate, and this is referred to as inflation.

Effects of Currency Inflation

Economists visualize currency inflation like the inflation of a balloon. A balloon that is filled with air appears to be growing, but the balloon itself is still very small. It only appears to be getting bigger because the air inside of it is stretching it into a large round shape. When there is too much air in a balloon, and it cannot stretch any further, it will pop. When the balloon pops, it becomes very clear that the balloon was not really growing at all, but that it remained basically unchanged since the inflation began, except that it got damaged in the process. Inflation is essentially the same process, as it applies to the debasement of a currency.

When an economy is experiencing inflation, everyone earns lots of money, but the prices are so high that the money is not technically worth as much. The nominal wages seem to be very high, but in reality, the real wages are a lot lower. This phenomenon will snowball and get exponentially worse until the government is forced to respond to it due to public outrage over the debasement of the currency.

In some countries where the governments let it go too far, citizens were forced to use foreign currencies or even bartering because the currency had no value. The expression "that's not worth the paper that it's printed on" comes from countries that had hyperinflation to the point where it cost more to print the money than the money was eventually worth. Hyperinflation reached levels so high that these currencies were totally undermined and had to be replaced. Such was the case in the following countries: France (1796), Austria (1922), Germany (1923), Soviet Union (1924), Greece (1944), Hungary (1946), China (1955), Poland (1923 and 1990), Yugoslavia (1994), Zimbabwe (2008). In all cases, hyperinflation results in a collapse of the currency, and usually a change in government, but fortunately, due to the efforts of central banks, this has been avoided in the developed world for several decades.

How Interest Rates Affect Investors

So when will interest rates rise? The unemployment rate is inversely related to inflation, and so the question of when interest rates will rise can be answered by first determining when the unemployment rate will drop. When the economy is overheating, inflation begins to rise, and it is at this point that the government will begin to remove stimulus and then apply the brakes in order to "cool the economy". When this decision is announced, everyone will understand that interest rates are rising. It is at this point that many established investors tend to move their investments away from riskier assets like the stock market and emerging markets, and back to the United States where the increased interest rates on treasury bills is expected to provide better return with lower risk.

As a by-product of this segment of the economic cycle, real estate prices may not be able to continue to rise because the rate of return on these investments will not be high enough to cover the higher borrowing costs. This means that when the economy is booming, interest rates will need to be raised, and this will put downward pressure on house prices as well as the stock market. Asset values will continue to experience downward pressure until it is noted that the economy needs to be stimulated once more. When investors all over the world are convinced that governments are acting together to stimulate the global economy, confidence in the markets is re-established and prices rise once again. This will happen when is known that the interest rates will be lowered. Lowering interest rates means that it will be slightly cheaper to borrow, and therefore more lucrative to invest in risky assets like stocks. This economic cycle continues to repeat itself time after time approximately every 10 to 20 years. It should be noted, however that historical behavior can never guarantee the future trends, and so nobody truly knows the precise timing of how the business cycle will unfold.

Why Variable Rate Mortgages Are Usually More Affordable

Defining a Variable Rate Mortgage

There are several reasons why a borrower might want to sign up for a variable rate mortgage instead of a fixed rate mortgage. Before elaborating, it is important to clarify a few definitions. An "open mortgage" has no maximum limit on monthly payments. A "closed mortgage" has a maximum limit on monthly payments, and this is most common. A "variable rate mortgage" is an arrangement where the interest rate moves up and down, according to the country's prime rate. A "fixed rate mortgage" is arranged so that the interest rate stays the same until the next renewal. This discussion focuses exclusively on fixed versus variable. Please note that variable rate mortgages are often referred to as "adjustable rate mortgages" or ARM's.

Fixed Rate Mortgages are an Up-Sell

Most people choose fixed rate mortgages because the banks succeed in convincing most borrowers that they should be fearful of the federal prime interest rate movements. This fear is not always justified. In most cases, increases in the federal prime interest rate are rare, minimal, and well-publicized in advance. Banks take on some risk by offering to fix the mortgage rate until the next renewal term. The fixed rate is therefore set so high that the bank will be covered if there is an unpredictable rise in the federal prime interest rate. Many banks still sell their fixed rate arrangements to a 3rd party global fund, such as a bond fund or mortgage-backed security fund. By selling the fixed payment contract, the bank is able to reduce some of their exposure to the risks of a federal interest rate fluctuation. Banks usually profit more on fixed rate mortgages because they charge such a hefty premium rate on the fixed rate option. The mortgage representative's objective is therefore to convince the borrower to pay as much interest as possible by fixing the mortgage.

Tactics to Encourage Fixed Rate Mortgages

The borrower will probably notice that the mortgage specialist will attempt to encourage them to select the fixed rate option every time, usually saying something along the lines of, *"You only pay 1% more, and you won't have to worry about rising payments."* First of all, one should definitely take a step back and think it over whenever a salesperson tries to scare them into signing up for anything. And secondly, according to the math, 1% is very significant for a mortgage balance. Even 0.5% is very expensive because most mortgage balances are hundreds of thousands of dollars.

In order to downplay the higher cost of fixing the mortgage, many banks resort to encouraging the borrower to renew with a term that is shorter than 5 years, sometimes as low as 2 years. In this arrangement, they can offer a slightly lower fixed rate because there is less probability that rates will rise significantly within 4 years versus 5 years. In order to clearly compare apples to apples, it is important to compare the 5 year fixed rate with the 5 year variable rate. A three or four year renewal term is a different product with different risk.

Another common trick the mortgage representatives use in order to downplay the higher cost of fixing the mortgage is to confuse the borrower by comparing the rate they are offering with the bank's prime rate. For example, they might say, *"I can sign you up for prime minus 40 basis points, so it's a discount."* The bank's prime rate is not the same as the federal prime rate. From the borrower's perspective, bank prime is meaningless, much like the pre-sale price of a pair of jeans. The words "discount" and "prime minus" are just sales tactics. The only rate that matters is the actual rate that the borrower will pay.

When Do Fixed Rate Mortgages Benefit the Borrower?

The only way a fixed mortgage is better for the borrower is if the borrower knows a massive secret about impending excessive national inflation, and none of the banks know about it. So, aside from hyperinflation, or something similar to the unprecedented baby-boomer-fuelled inflation in the 1980's, the borrower pays more overall interest almost every time by signing up for a fixed rate mortgage. At this point, to be fair, it is important to provide a necessary disclaimer.

It must be admitted that there is indeed a risk that all variable rate borrowers must face. From the time of signing until the time of renewal, which is 5 years for most people, anything can happen in this crazy world. There is a possibility that the borrower's rate will go up more than 1% within the 5 year term. If that happens in the 5th year, the borrower still might end up paying less overall interest, but rates could go up much higher unexpectedly quickly.

This rare situation would amount to a massive shock to all borrowers around the world, from home-owners to governments to banks. As they say on Wall Street, you need to take a risk in order to get your reward, or in other words, "Either you eat well, or you sleep well." The only caveat that can be provided about this scenario is that both the fixed and variable borrowers would have to face those higher rates when they renew in any case, and so the fixed rate can only protect the borrower for a few years until the next renewal. At this point, we can return to the discussion pertaining to the borrower's advantages in selecting the variable rate option.

How to Change the Terms of the Mortgage Beforehand

An interesting way to determine how the mortgage representative's commission is arranged is to watch what they encourage, and how they react when their suggestions are not followed. For example, this can be seen by telling the mortgage sales representative that the borrower believes the federal prime interest rate will not likely rise higher than the bank's fixed rate within the next 5 year renewal term. The sales representative will probably become visibly irate and/or disappointed, almost taking it personally, as though they earn a higher commission on the up-sell to the fixed option. In fact, it might be necessary to provide this reason to the rep, in order to convince them that they can stop trying to aggressively sell the fixed rate option.

As a borrower, it can be stressful to be exposed to future increases in the monthly mortgage payments. There is a way, however, to get the lower variable rate without having to put up with fluctuating monthly payments. Simply put, if the borrower opts for the variable rate, some banks still offer the option to fix the monthly payment amount. Mortgage contracts are more flexible than most people think. Few people are aware of this option, because mortgage representatives do not have a tendency to mention this possibility, and so it is up to the borrower to inquire about this arrangement.

This option means that if the federal prime interest rate increases by 0.25%, for example, the borrower will be exposed to a rate increase, because in the background, slightly less of the monthly payment will go towards paying down the principal. However, in return for taking on this risk, the borrower will be able to have their mortgage set up with the much lower variable interest rate, and at the same time, they will not have to worry about their monthly payments going up. It should be noted that the fear of a rising monthly payment is half of the reason why most people are convinced that they should select the expensive fixed rate option to begin with. And just to clarify the benefits of a variable rate even further, if the federal prime interest rate drops, the borrower's rate will drop as well, meaning more of their monthly payment will go towards paying down the mortgage balance. If the federal prime interest rate stays the same, the borrower still wins because they are avoiding the higher fixed rate.

So before a borrower goes into the mortgage rep's office to negotiate the terms of their very expensive mortgage contract, they should shop around with at least 10 lenders, and as part of their research, it is important to ask if the bank in question is willing to sign them up for the variable rate option but with a fixed monthly payment. More likely than not, they will agree to it before the borrower even visits them in person, because even though they are unable to up-sell the borrower into the fixed rate option, they know that they can still earn a commission with a mortgage that is arranged to benefit the borrower in this manner. Otherwise, they know that there are many competing banks who will gladly offer those terms, in order to gain a new customer.

A Hidden Fee in the Mortgage Contract

There's a rather dubious penalty fee that many lenders will sneak into the mortgage contract, mentioning it to the borrower in the last moment when it's time to sign. If at all possible, it is worth the effort to try to negotiate this trap-like clause out of the contract. This is basically a fee of whatever amount the bank wants to charge, often a few hundred dollars, that the borrower must pay if they diligently shop around and switch to another lender at the time of renewal.

The borrower should ask about this on the phone or by email before meeting the mortgage representative in person. It is often non-negotiable, so the only way to avoid it is to avoid meeting with banks that charge this fee. It can be found in a section of the contract called "Other Charges," or elsewhere. If this is left in the contract, then in a few years, the bank will unscrupulously charge this ridiculous fee of a couple hundred dollars in an attempt to prevent the borrower from leaving the bank for a lender who offers a competitive rate. Please note that there may also be a nominal government fee for assigning a mortgage to another lender upon renewal as well, which may be unavoidable. In any case, not all banks charge this fee, so it is worthwhile to ask in advance.

Disclaimer

Please note that the purpose of this book is primarily to increase awareness of certain real estate considerations. The reader is advised to perform further research to assess the value of real estate and to decide on the relevance of the clauses in their mortgage contract. Due to the sensitive nature and risk involved in real estate and other investments, the reader is strongly encouraged to consult a licensed financial advisor and local real estate professional for more guidance that is specific to their unique individual situation.

Appendix: Valuation Indicator Summary Worksheet

Price/Income Ratio

_____ Average home price within a local property market (A)
_____ Average income within the same property market (B)
_____ Average price/income ratio (A ÷ B)

_____ Price of property being considered for purchase (C)
_____ Total household income (D)
_____ Household price/income ratio (C ÷ D)

If the price/income ratio is greater than 3, then the household may struggle to afford the home. If this ratio approaches 7, the household will likely spend most of their income exclusively on the mortgage.

Vacancy Rate

_____ Vacancy rate within the local property market

A vacancy rate that is higher than 5% is an indication that there may be an over-supply of rental units in the local real estate market.

Price/Earnings Ratio

_____ Property Price (E)
÷____ Annual Rent (F)
=____ Basic Price/Earnings Ratio (E ÷ F)

_____ Property Price (G)
-____ Legal Fees (H)
-____ Land Transfer Taxes (I)
-____ Other Purchase Fees (J)
=____ (K) = Adjusted price (G – H – I – J)

_____ Annual rent for a similar property (L)
-____ Annual mortgage interest (M) Interest Rate x Balance
-____ Annual property taxes (N)
-____ Other annual costs to rent the property to a tenant (O)
=____ (P) = Potential annual earnings (L – M – N – O)

____% Return on Investment Percentage (P ÷ K x 100)
_____ Price / Earnings Ratio (K ÷ P x 100)

Approximate guidelines for the property value according to the potential rental earnings:
_____ Minimum price that the seller would accept (P x 14)
_____ Maximum price that the buyer would offer (P x 18)

www.ingramcontent.com/pod-product-compliance
Lightning Source LLC
Chambersburg PA
CBHW031524210526
45464CB00007B/3023